# A New True Book

# REPTILES

### By Lois Ballard

This "true book" was prepared
under the direction of
Illa Podendorf,
formerly with the Laboratory School,
University of Chicago

CHILDRENS PRESS, CHICAGO

Chuckwalla lizard

PHOTO CREDITS

Reinhard Brucker—2, 45 (top left)

Lynn M. Stone—Cover, 4, 7 (2 photos), 10 (right), 14
(left), 15, 16 (2 photos), 17 (2 photos), 19 (top), 20, 22
(top), 24, (2 photos), 32, 35 (left), 42 (bottom), 45 (bottom)

James P. Rowan—8, 14 (right), 21 (2 photos), 23, 37, 45
(top right)

Allan Roberts—10 (left), 11, 22 (bottom), 25, 26, 27
(3 photos), 28, 29 (2 photos), 31, 35 (right), 36, 39
(2 photos), 41, 42 (top), 44

Bill Thomas Photo—12, 19 (bottom), 34, 40

COVER—American crocodile

Library of Congress Cataloging in Publication Data

Ballard, Lois.
  Reptiles.

  (A New true book)
  Previously published as: The true book of
reptiles. 1957.
  Summary: A brief introduction to the cold-
blooded, backboned, lung-breathing, scaled
animals known as reptiles, which include
turtles, lizards, alligators, crocodiles, and
snakes.
  1. Reptiles—Juvenile literature.
[1. Reptiles]  I.  Title.
QL665.B34    1982      597.9      81-38525
ISBN 0-516-01644-X       AACR2

# TABLE OF CONTENTS

Iguana

# REPTILES ARE ANIMALS

Animals need food.
Animals need air.
Animals grow.
Animals make more
animals like themselves.
Reptiles are animals.
Reptiles need food and
air, and they grow.
Reptiles make more
reptiles like themselves.

Anole

Monitor lizard

# HOW REPTILES ARE ALIKE

All reptiles have backbones.

All reptiles breathe with lungs.

All reptiles have scales on the outside of their bodies.

Many animals have backbones, but they are not reptiles.

Many animals have lungs, but they are not reptiles.

Many animals have scales, but they are not reptiles.

Fish have scales, but are not reptiles.

Only reptiles have
backbones, lungs, and
scales, and are cold-
blooded.

All reptiles are cold-
blooded animals. They are
no warmer than the air
around them. When the air
is cold, they are cold.
When the air is warm, they
are warm.

Most reptiles live in
warm places.

No reptiles live where it
is cold all of the time.

A rough green snake lays eggs.

A baby turtle hatches.

# REPTILE BABIES

Baby reptiles hatch from eggs.

Many kinds of reptiles lay their eggs in warm places.

A copperhead snake's babies are born live, not hatched.

A few kinds of reptiles keep their eggs in their bodies until the eggs hatch. Then the babies are born. Soon they learn to look after themselves.

Baby alligators

Baby reptiles look much like their mothers and fathers. Some kinds of reptiles change colors as they grow up.

# REPTILES WITH SHELLS ON THEIR BACKS

Turtles are reptiles.

Turtle shells are made of scales.

There are many kinds of turtles.

Some kinds live on land and some live in water.

Mud turtle

Snapping turtle

Mud turtles live in mud.
They are not easy to see.
They are the same color
as the mud.

Snapping turtles live in
water. They eat fish and
plants.

Box turtle

Box turtles live on land.
Their bottom shells can
move. They are able to
close themselves like
boxes. This helps protect
them.

Box turtles eat insects, worms, and berries.

Soft-shelled turtles have soft shells. They are flat like pancakes. Some people think that they are good to eat.

Sea turtles live in the ocean.

A soft-shelled turtle's long nose helps it breathe when it is underwater.

Left:
The loggerhead
turtle lives in
the sea.

Below:
A desert tortoise
lives on land.

They grow to be very
big. A sea turtle may
weigh as much as a horse.
Desert tortoises live in
dry places.

# REPTILES WITH FOUR LEGS
# THAT LIVE ON LAND

Lizards are reptiles.

Most lizards have four legs and live on land.

One kind of lizard has a funny name. It is a skink. Most skinks have long smooth bodies and small legs. They hide under flat stones and logs.

The American chameleon is a lizard.

Chameleon

It can change color. It
can change from brown or
yellow to green. It eats
mealworms, flies, and other
insects.

Horned toad

Horned toads are lizards
with horns on their heads.
They live where it is very
warm and dry.
They are harmless.

Velvet gecko

Leopard gecko

A gecko is a lizard with little pads on its toes. The pads help it hold on to smooth places.

It can walk upside down. A gecko eats insects.

Fence swifts are hard to catch, because they run so very fast. They eat worms and many kinds of insects.

Tuataras are a different kind of reptile. A tuatara looks like a lizard. But tuataras are thought to be like dinosaurs of long ago.

A fence swift

Tuataras live only in New Zealand.

American alligator

# REPTILES WITH FOUR LEGS THAT LIVE IN WATER

Alligators and crocodiles are reptiles that live in warm water. So do gavials and caimans.

23

Above: Gavial
Left: American crocodile

They all look very much alike. But crocodiles and gavials have more pointed noses.

These reptiles lay their eggs on land.

When they grow up, these reptiles can be longer than a man is tall.

Albino corn snake

# REPTILES WITH NO LEGS

Snakes are reptiles.
They do not have legs.
Snakes can move very
fast.

They have scales and muscles on the undersides of their bodies. The scales and muscles help them move.

All snakes are able to swallow things much bigger than themselves.

They can open their mouths very wide. The lower jaw spreads apart.

Some snakes
eat other snakes.

Some snakes
eat birds.

Some snakes
eat fish. After
snakes eat, they
spit out the
animal parts that
their bodies
cannot use.

Cobra

Snakes run their tongues
in and out very fast. They
cannot hurt anything with
their tongues. They are
only finding out more
about the world around
them. Their tongues help
them smell things.

Snakes often push against rough
things to get off their old skins.

As a snake grows, it
gets too big for its skin. It
sheds the old skin. Then it
has a new one underneath.

# ALL KINDS OF SNAKES

Many kinds of snakes
are helpful.

Some kinds are the
farmer's friends.

They eat rats and mice.

Rats and mice eat the
farmer's grain. A farmer
does not want these pests.

Milk
snake

Milk snakes eat mice
from barns and corn cribs.
Milk snakes never drink
milk. People once thought
that they drank milk, so
they named them milk
snakes.

A corn snake squeezes a mouse before eating it.

The corn snake and the milk snake are constrictors. They are called constrictors because of the way they catch their food.

They wind their long bodies around the small animals which they catch. They squeeze the animals so that they cannot breathe. Then the snakes swallow the animals whole.

Bull snakes are constrictors, too. They are very big snakes. Some of them grow to be nine feet long.

Hog-nosed snake

A hog-nosed snake makes noises and acts mean. It is really very gentle. Sometimes it rolls over on its back and acts as though it were dead.

Racer snakes got their name because they move so fast. They can also climb trees.

Garter snakes are striped. They are harmless.

Garter snakes eat insects, worms, and frogs. There are several kinds of garter snakes.

Some snakes are not easy to see.

Green grass snakes look like the green grass.

Left: Garter snake
Below: Green snake

Some snakes look like a tree branch.

King snakes look like the ground.

King snakes are helpful. They eat other kinds of snakes that are not our friends.

King snake

Prairie rattlesnake

# POISONOUS SNAKES

The snakes you have been reading about are harmless and helpful.

A few kinds of snakes are poisonous.

The real difference is in their mouths.

Harmless snakes have rows of short, pointed teeth. Their teeth help them catch and hold food.

Poisonous snakes have long, hollow teeth called fangs.

Poisonous snakes bite with these fangs. Poison runs through them.

Diamond-back rattlesnake

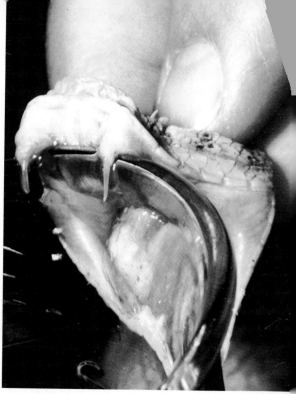
The fangs of a poisonous snake

All rattlesnakes are poisonous.

All of them have rattles at the end of their tails.

There are several kinds of rattlesnakes.

A water moccasin is poisonous.

It lives in or near water.

When a water moccasin opens its mouth, it looks as though there were cotton inside. So they are sometimes called cottonmouths.

Cottonmouth, or water moccasin

Copperhead snake

The copperhead snake is poisonous.

It is wise to play safe and let a snake alone, unless you are sure it is a harmless one.

# Sometimes it is hard to tell which snakes are poisonous.

Two harmless snakes, the bull snake (top) and the scarlet king snake (below)

A harmless bull snake sometimes moves its tail very fast against leaves and twigs. He makes a sound like a rattlesnake. This sound fools people. They think it is a rattlesnake.

Coral snakes look a great deal like scarlet king snakes.

But the coral snake has
fangs, and is poisonous.
The scarlet king snake has
short teeth, and is
harmless.

The common water
snake is not poisonous.
But sea snakes are
poisonous.

Sea snake

Top left: Collared lizard
Above: Bearded dragon lizards
Left: Water snake

There are many kinds of reptiles. Some of them help us. Some are harmful. All have their place in nature.

# WORDS YOU SHOULD KNOW

**alligator**(AL•ih•gay•ter) —a large four-legged reptile with a broad head that lives near water in hot, wet places

**backbone** —the main bone of a body; the spine

**caiman**(kay•MAN) —a large four-legged reptile much like an alligator that lives in Central and South America

**chameleon**(kuh•MEEL•yun) —a lizard that can change color

**constrictor**(kun•STRIHK•ter) —a type of snake that kills its food by squeezing

**crib** —a small building used for storing corn and other grains

**crocodile**(KRAHK•uh•dyl) —a large four-legged reptile with a narrow nose or snout that lives near water in hot, wet places

**gavial**(GAY•vee•uhl) —a large four-legged reptile with long, thin jaws that lives near water in India

**harmless** —not doing harm

**hollow**(HOLL•oh) —having an empty space inside

**lizard**(LIZ•erd) —a reptile with four legs that lives on land

**lung** —the part of an animal's body used in breathing

**moccasin**(MAHK•uh•sin) —a poisonous snake that lives in or near water; a cottonmouth snake

**poisonous**(POY•zun•us) —full of something that can harm or kill a living thing

**reptile**(REHP•tyl) —a cold-blooded animal with lungs, scales, and a backbone

**scale**(SKAYL) —a small, thin part that makes up the skin of fish and reptiles

**tuatara**(tyu•ah•TEHR•uh) —a lizard-like reptile that lives in New Zealand

# INDEX

## About the Author

*Lois Ballard is a school librarian in Norfolk, Virginia. Her book on reptiles grew out of a project in a graduate course in reading at the University of Virginia — subject matter presented in simple vocabulary, that interests first graders and reluctant readers in higher grades.*